7/13

What are stems?

by Molly Aloian

 Crabtree Publishing Company
www.crabtreebooks.com

Author
Molly Aloian

Publishing plan research and development
Sean Charlebois, Reagan Miller
Crabtree Publishing Company

Editors
Reagan Miller, Crystal Sikkens

Proofreader
Kathy Middleton

Notes to adults
Reagan Miller

Photo research
Allison Napier, Ken Wright, Crystal Sikkens

Design
Ken Wright

Production coordinator and Prepress technician
Ken Wright

Print coordinator
Katherine Berti

Photographs
Dreamstime: page 16
Thinkstock: title page, pages 7, 9, 11, 14, 15, 19, 21, 23
Shutterstock: pages 4, 5, 6, 8, 10, 12, 13, 18
Wikimedia Commons: Kumar83: page 17
Other images by Thinkstock

Library and Archives Canada Cataloguing in Publication

Aloian, Molly
  What are stems? / Molly Aloian.

(Plants close-up)
Includes index.
Issued also in electronic formats.
ISBN 978-0-7787-4222-7 (bound).--ISBN 978-0-7787-4227-2 (pbk.)

  1. Stems (Botany)--Juvenile literature. 2. Plant anatomy--Juvenile literature. I. Title. II. Series: Plants close-up

QK646.A46 2012   j581.4'95   C2012-900403-0

Library of Congress Cataloging-in-Publication Data

Aloian, Molly.
  What are stems? / Molly Aloian.
      p. cm. -- (Plants close-up)
  Includes index.
  ISBN 978-0-7787-4222-7 (reinforced library binding : alk. paper) --
ISBN 978-0-7787-4227-2 (pbk. : alk. paper) -- ISBN 978-1-4271-7907-4
(electronic pdf) -- ISBN 978-1-4271-8022-3 (electronic html)
  1. Stems (Botany)--Juvenile literature. I. Title.

QK646.A46 2012
581.4'95--dc23
                                              2012001125

Crabtree Publishing Company

www.crabtreebooks.com   1-800-387-7650

Printed in the USA/052013/JA20130412

Published in Canada
Crabtree Publishing
616 Welland Ave.
St. Catharines, Ontario
L2M 5V6

Published in the United States
Crabtree Publishing
PMB 59051
350 Fifth Avenue, 59th Floor
New York, New York 10118

Published in the United Kingdom
Crabtree Publishing
Maritime House
Basin Road North, Hove
BN41 1WR

Published in Australia
Crabtree Publishing
3 Charles Street
Coburg North
VIC 3058

Contents

Plants have stems

Plants are living things. They need nutrients, air, sunlight, and water to stay alive.

flower

stem

leaves

roots

Plants have stems. They also have roots and leaves. Some have flowers. Each plant part has a job to do to help the plant stay alive.

Different stems

Some plants have very long stems.

Others have short stems.

Some plants have thick, tough stems.

Other plants have thin stems that bend easily.

Some stems are soft and smooth.

Other stems are rough.

A stem's jobs

A plant's stem supports the leaves and flowers. It holds the leaves and flowers up so they get plenty of sunlight.

Water and nutrients enter through the roots and travel up the plant's stem. The stem carries the water and nutrients to the leaves and flowers.

Storing water

Some plants grow in dry places with little rain.

The plants store water and nutrients in their stems to use when they cannot get them from the soil.

stem

This cactus plant has thick, green stems for storing water and nutrients.

Neat nodes

nodes

The place where a leaf, twig, or root comes out of a stem is called a **node**. There are usually many nodes on a stem.

leaf scar

One or more leaves grow from each node. When a leaf drops off a plant, it leaves a mark called a scar on the stem.

Best buds

leaf bud

Buds grow from the nodes on a stem. A bud is a
shoot that is ready to grow into a leaf or flower.

A bud also grows at the very tip of a stem.

flower bud

Stem cuttings

Part of a plant's stem can be cut off and planted to grow a new plant. The part that is cut off is called a **cutting**.

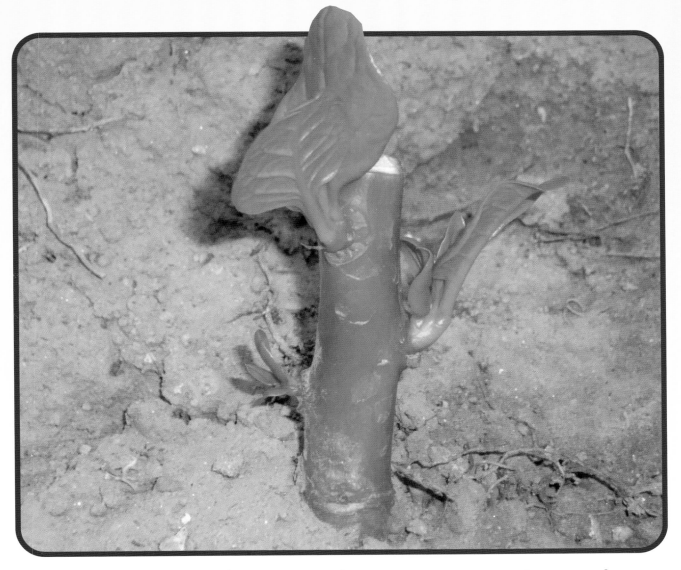

A cutting must have at least one node and a few leaves in order to grow into a new plant.

Underground stems

potato stem

potato bud

Some plants have stems that grow under the ground. Potatoes are underground stems. The stems have buds that grow into new potatoes.

The leaves of a potato plant grow above the ground. They take in the sunlight and air that the plant needs to live.

potato leaves

Stay away!

thorn

Some plants have stems with **thorns** or other protective parts. Thorns help to protect the plants from being eaten by hungry animals.

The thorns on this rose stem will protect the plant from animals that get too close.

Seeing stems

There are stems all around you!

Did you know that tree **trunks** are stems?

Some trees, like this redwood tree, have trunks as big around as your bedroom!

Words to know

buds 14-15

cutting 16-17

node 12-13, 14

thorns
20-21

trunks
22-23

Notes for adults and an experiment

How does water travel through a plant?

• Instructions to adults: Use a knife to cut the stem of a white carnation at a 45° angle. Help children fill a glass jar with water and add 20 drops of food dye to the water. Stir until the dye is dissolved. Ask children to predict what will happen to the carnation when placed in the colored water. Place the flower in the water and have children record their observations a few hours later and also the following day.

• Recording Observations: Encourage children to write their observations in a science journal. They can also draw pictures or take photographs of the flower to add to their journal. Discuss with children why the flower changed color. What did they learn about how water travels through a plant?

Learning More

Books

How do plants help us? (My World) by Bobbie Kalman. Crabtree Publishing Company (2011)
A Bean s Life (Crabtree Connections) by Angela Royston. Crabtree Publishing Company (2011)

Websites

The Great Plant Escape: Children team up with Detective LePlant to identify plant parts and functions and explore how a plant grows.
http://urbanext.illinois.edu/gpe/index.cfm

Michigan 4-H Children's Garden Tour: This interactive site takes visitors on a virtual garden tour. Children learn about different kinds of plants, play educational games, and answer questions.
http://4hgarden.msu.edu/kidstour/tour.html